PROBLEM SOLVED!
YOUR TURN TO THINK BIG

Innovations in Safety

CYNTHIA O'BRIEN

Crabtree Publishing Company
www.crabtreebooks.com

Crabtree Publishing Company
www.crabtreebooks.com

Author: Cynthia O'Brien

Series research and development: Reagan Miller

Editorial director: Kathy Middleton

Editors: Crystal Sikkens, Janine Deschenes

Proofreader: Petrice Custance

Designer: Ken Wright

Cover design: Ken Wright

Photo researchers: Ken Wright, Crystal Sikkens

**Production coordinator
and prepress technician:** Ken Wright

Print coordinator: Katherine Berti

Photographs:

Alamy: ZUMA Press Inc, p 7;

Getty Images: JEFF KOWALSKY / Stringer, p 14 (right); Bloomberg, p 19 (top left); Bennett Raglin / Stringer, p 25

iStock: © Teemu Tretjakov, p 17

Revolights: p 13

Shutterstock: © Sean Nel, p 10

Superstock: The Francis Frith Collection, p 23

Thinkstock: Hemera Technologies, p 9 (bkgd);

Wikimedia: cover (bottom right); p 6 (bkgd); p 8 (top right); Joshuavr, p 12 (bottom left); United States public domain, p 22 (top right)

All other images by Shutterstock

Cover: (background) The windshield wiper; (left) Fluorescent colors for safety vests; (top right) Life jackets; (bottom right) The safety helmet

Title page: The sports safety helmet has changed over time as new, stronger materials were invented.

Library and Archives Canada Cataloguing in Publication

O'Brien, Cynthia (Cynthia J.), author
    Innovations in safety / Cynthia O'Brien.

(Problem solved! your turn to think big)
Includes index.
Issued in print and electronic formats.
ISBN 978-0-7787-2679-1 (hardback).--
ISBN 978-0-7787-2685-2 (paperback).--
ISBN 978-1-4271-1806-6 (html)

    1. Industrial safety--Technological innovations--Juvenile literature. 2. Accidents--Prevention--Juvenile literature. 3. Inventions--Juvenile literature. I. Title.

T55.O27 2016   j363.1   C2016-904157-3
                                     C2016-904158-1

Library of Congress Cataloging-in-Publication Data

Names: O'Brien, Cynthia (Cynthia J.), author.
Title: Innovations in safety / Cynthia O'Brien.
Description: New York, NY : Crabtree Publishing Company, [2016] | Series: Problem solved! Your turn to think big | Includes index.
Identifiers: LCCN 2016026663 (print) | LCCN 2016030064 (ebook) | ISBN 9780778726791 (reinforced library binding) | ISBN 9780778726852 (pbk.) | ISBN 9781427118066 (Electronic HTML)
Subjects: LCSH: Industrial safety--Juvenile literature. | Human security--Juvenile literature.
Classification: LCC T55 .O2285 2016 (print) | LCC T55 (ebook) | DDC 363.1--dc23
LC record available at https://lccn.loc.gov/2016026663

Crabtree Publishing Company
www.crabtreebooks.com   1-800-387-7650

Printed in Canada/102016/IH20160811

**Published in Canada
Crabtree Publishing**
616 Welland Ave.
St. Catharines, Ontario
L2M 5V6

**Published in the United States
Crabtree Publishing**
PMB 59051
350 Fifth Avenue, 59th Floor
New York, New York 10118

**Published in the United Kingdom
Crabtree Publishing**
Maritime House
Basin Road North, Hove
BN41 1WR

**Published in Australia
Crabtree Publishing**
3 Charles Street
Coburg North
VIC, 3058

CONTENTS

Keeping Safe

All around us are **inventions** and **innovations** that keep us safe. What happens if you fall off your bike? You can hurt your head! Luckily, inventors created a bike helmet long before you started riding bikes. Other inventors have made driving on our roads safer. Garret Morgan invented traffic lights to help drivers know when to stop and go.

Inventors and innovators solve a problem or meet a need. Look around you. Do you see anything that seems unsafe? Maybe you will create the next great safety invention or innovation!

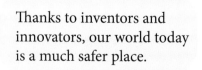

Thanks to inventors and innovators, our world today is a much safer place.

Inventors and Innovators

An inventor creates a product or process that did not exist before. The first seatbelt was an invention. An innovator changes or improves on an invention that already exists. Nils Bohlin was an innovator that improved the seat belt design to create the three-point seat belt, which we use today.

An **engineer's** job is to use science and math to solve problems or meet needs. Sometimes, engineers can also be inventors and innovators, when they make new solutions or improve on existing ones. Inventors, innovators, and engineers all share the same **traits**, such as curiosity and creativity.

Today's three-point seat belt is an example of an innovation. The lap and shoulder belts are connected so you can buckle both with one motion.

Safe Inside

Before the smoke alarm, thousands of people died every year from fires in their homes. It was especially hard for people to survive fires when they started at night, when people were sleeping. The best idea to solve this problem happened by accident. In the 1930s, Walter Jaeger was building a device to detect poisonous gas. Unfortunately, his experiments weren't working. Frustrated, he stopped to light a cigarette and something happened—his device detected the smoke! This led to the first smoke alarm. Later, innovators Duane Pearsall and Stanley B. Peterson created the battery-operated, smoke-detecting alarm that we use today.

Today, most homes have smoke alarms. This important invention has saved many lives.

Safety without Noise

People who are **hearing-impaired** often can't hear ordinary smoke alarms. To solve this problem, hearing-impaired Barbara and Sidney Anders created alert systems that will wake a sleeping person. These devices can help save the lives of hearing-impaired people during a fire.

Hearing-impaired people can install devices such as a bedside fire alarm. It flashes the word "FIRE" and triggers a bed shaker located under the mattress. The bed then vibrates and shakes, waking the person in case of a fire.

Breathing Safely

Imagine if firefighters had nothing to protect them from smoke. How could they help us when there is a fire? According to stories, some firefighters used to wet their long beards and use them as smoke screens. This proved to be unsuccessful. It was only after James Braidwood invented special breathing equipment that firefighters could do their job more easily. Braidwood, being a firefighter himself, knew that smoke from any kind of fire is **toxic**. To help with this, he designed a leather mask with hoses that attached to an air-filled bag. This invention helped firefighters to breathe safely in smoke-filled buildings.

Innovations have improved Braidwood's breathing equipment. Today, firefighters use light breathing masks that have built-in alarms and radio systems.

Putting Out the Fire

Small fires in your home or school can sometimes be put out by using a fire extinguisher. This **portable** safety device was designed in 1813 by inventor George Manby. Manby's first fire extinguisher was made from a 3-gallon (11-liter) copper tank that shot a special salt water solution through a small hose onto a burning fire.

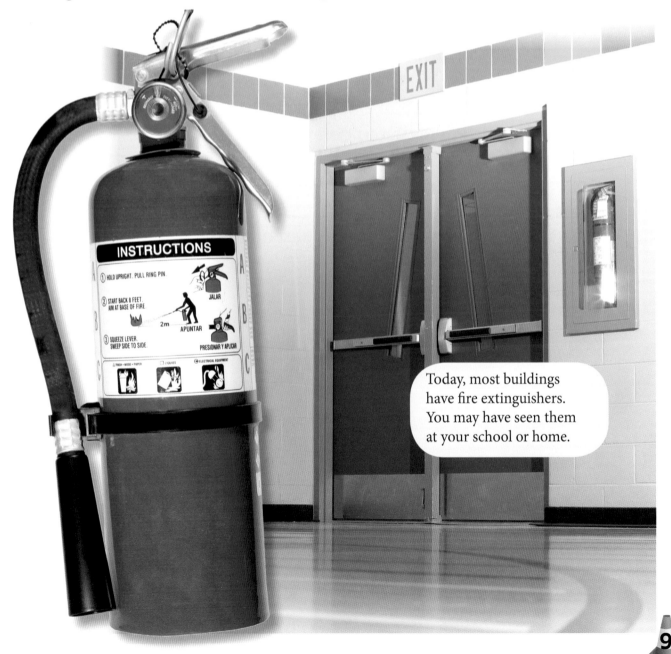

Today, most buildings have fire extinguishers. You may have seen them at your school or home.

Dressed for Safety

Our clothes protect our skin. If you fall, long pants or a long-sleeve shirt might prevent you from getting scrapes or cuts. Some people, such as police officers, firefighters, and soldiers, need more protection than just everyday clothes. They wear special clothing made of a fabric known as Kevlar to protect them in their dangerous jobs. Kevlar fabric is five times stronger than steel, does not tear, and can withstand high temperatures. Chemist Stephanie Kwolek initally invented this strong material for use on car tires. Before long, police officers, firefighters, and soldiers began wearing it as part of their uniforms.

Police officers wear bulletproof vests made from Kevlar.

Motorcycle riders often wear clothing made of Kevlar to protect them if they fall.

The DayGlo Brothers

Crossing guards, construction workers, and even runners or bikers often wear **fluorescent** clothing that helps drivers see them easily. This special clothing got its start in the 1930s, when 19-year-old Bob Switzer had an accident that damaged his eyes, requiring him to recover in a dark room. During that time, he and his brother, Joseph, experimented with colors that became much brighter when placed under **black light**. Over the years, the brothers also created colors that glowed brighter in daylight, and ones that glowed in regular darkness. They began selling their fluorescent colors and paints under the company name Switzer Bros. Today, we know the company as DayGlo Color Corp.

Thanks to DayGlo, fluorescent clothing can be easily seen both during the day and at night.

On Two Wheels

Decades ago, cyclists wore nothing to protect their heads in case of bicycle accidents. To help reduce the numbers of serious injuries, the first bicycle helmet was invented in 1975. While bike helmets keep riders safe, some people complain that they are uncomfortable to wear. To fix this problem, Swedish university students Anna Haupt and Terese Alton set out to make a comfortable helmet. Their innovation, called Hövding, looks like a collar that is worn around the rider's neck. If an accident occurs, the Hövding inflates before the rider falls, turning the collar into a big, puffy helmet that protects the rider's head and neck.

The Hövding is the first airbag for cyclists!

Lighting the Way

Bike lights are another invention that help cyclists stay safe in the dark. Revolight is one of the latest innovations in night safety. The Revolight team, led by Kent Frankovich and Bryan Duggan, developed white lights for the front bicycle wheel to help the rider see the road ahead and warn oncoming traffic. Red lights on the back wheel alert drivers from behind.

Lights attached to the wheels, which are low to the ground, make it easier for a rider to see obstacles on the road.

Drive Safely

The first cars were open carriages. The roads were very bumpy, so people used ropes and straps to stay in their seats. These were the first seat belts. If you ride in a car today, you wear a modern seat belt. However, even fifty years ago, most people found seat belts uncomfortable and difficult to use. Around this time, Nils Bohlin, a safety engineer, had an amazing idea. He designed a "three-point" seat belt that would provide better safety and comfort. Since then, Bohlin's innovation has saved millions of lives.

Nils Bohlin (right) created the seat belt design that we use today. It has a strap across the hips and one across the body.

Young Inventor Spotlight

Alissa Chavez

On hot days, it is even hotter inside a car. Alissa Chavez heard stories about children left in hot cars by accident. Some children died from the heat. To help with this problem, Alissa invented the Hot Seat Alarm. If the parent walks more than 33 feet (10 meters) away from the child in the car, an alarm will go off in the car, as well as on the parent's cell phone or a device attached to the parent's key chain. This will remind the parent that their child is still in the hot car.

On average, 37 children die each year in the United States from being left in a hot car. Hopefully, with the help of young inventors such as Alissa, these deaths can be avoided.

Soft Landing

Over fifty years ago, John Hetrick was driving with his wife and daughter when suddenly he noticed a large rock on the road. He made a sharp turn and ended up in the ditch. Both John and his wife had to reach out to stop themselves and their daughter from hitting the dashboard and steering wheel. Luckily, the family was uninjured, but many people can get badly hurt when their face or head hits the dashboard in an accident. To prevent this, John Hetrick decided to invent the first "airbag," which would inflate in an accident and provide a cushion between the passengers and the steering wheel and dashboard.

Innovations over the years have improved the speed at which an airbag inflates. This has helped keep people safer in accidents.

Safety Glass

Years ago, if a car was involved in an accident, the windshield would often shatter, sending sharp pieces of glass flying into the car, and harming the people inside. To fix this problem, Edouard Benedictus invented safety glass, which is made of two layers of glass with a layer of plastic in between. The plastic helps to hold the broken glass in place during an accident, which prevents the passengers from being harmed by flying glass.

It is also more difficult for objects to go through safety glass.

Stop!

Today, traffic lights give us even more information, such as signals to tell us when it is safe to walk.

Traffic lights tell drivers what to do at an **intersection**. Long ago, people actually operated the lights to turn them red for "stop," and green for "go." Notice anything missing? William Potts, a police officer, had seen many accidents in which cars were unable to stop in time when the light turned red. Potts figured that if drivers had a warning signal that the light was about to turn red, there would be fewer accidents. His innovation? He added an amber, or yellow, light! The amber light warns drivers they should start preparing to stop.

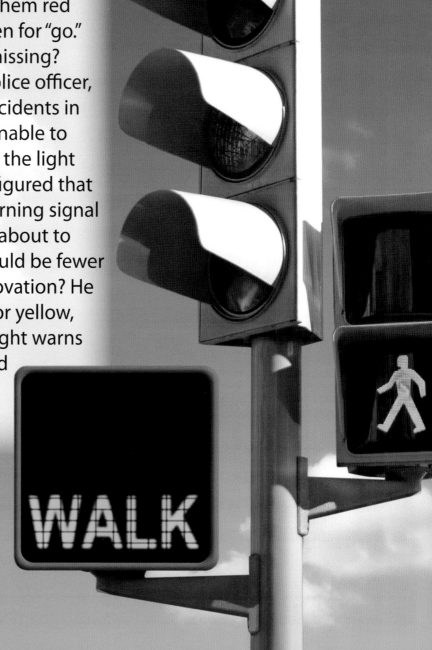

WALK

Young Inventor
Spotlight

T.J. Evarts

The SMARTWheel can easily attach to any steering wheel to help improve driving habits.

Inventors and innovators today are making driving safer than ever. When T.J. Evarts was a teenager, he noticed that many drivers were distracted by cell phones, the radio, and other things. Distracted drivers were causing thousands of accidents. To help make the roads safer, Evarts invented the SMARTWheel. This smart invention is a steering wheel cover that senses when one of the driver's hands is removed from the wheel. Lights and sound then alert the driver, and help bring their focus back to the road.

In Clear Sight

Driving through rain and snow used to be a big problem. Drivers could not see where they were going! They often had to stop and brush off the rain or snow. **Streetcar** drivers sometimes drove with their heads out the window. This wasn't very safe! In 1903, Mary Anderson decided to help with this problem by inventing a "window-cleaning device." It included a wood and rubber arm that the driver could turn on from inside the vehicle.

Mary Anderson's invention led to the modern windshield wipers we use today.

Young Inventor Spotlight

Charles F. Johnson

Driving during bad weather can be dangerous, but inventors and innovators are making it easier to be safe. In winter, ice on bridges takes a long time to melt, making them dangerous places for drivers. When he was 12 years old, Charles F. Johnson invented a device to melt bridge ice. It uses **solar power** to pump warm water or electricity onto the bridge surface, so icy bridge roads are made safe and dry again.

Charles's driving safety inventions didn't stop there. Two years later, he designed a train-detecting device. It warns car drivers near train crossings that a train is on the track.

On the Water

The first people to think about water safety were sailors. Sailing in rough seas meant **shipwrecks** were common. Even strong swimmers drowned in stormy, cold water. They had nothing to help them stay afloat. This changed, however, when Captain John Ross Ward invented the life jacket in 1851.

Today, we wear a life jacket whenever we are on a boat or want to feel safe in the water.

Cork Vest

Ward wanted to design something to protect lifeboat crews in water. Lifeboat crews helped to rescue people from shipwrecks or other water disasters. Ward did some experiments and discovered that cork floated in water. So, he designed a cork vest for crews to wear. Over time, innovators thought of ways to improve Ward's design. Now, life jackets keep us afloat with the use of air or plastic foam.

People wore Ward's cork life jacket design for almost 100 years.

Safety for Everyone

Inventors have come up with great ideas to solve problems for people with **disabilities**. People who are blind often need a cane to help them walk. Innovators have found a way to improve the cane by creating a device known as the "SmartCane." This invention attaches to a cane and beeps when it senses objects in the way. The iAid belt, invented by Alex Deans, is another device that works in a similar way. The belt has four sensors that scan the surroundings. A joystick held by the user moves to direct them around any obstacles.

A person that is blind uses a cane that looks like a white and red stick. With the cane, they can feel if there are any obstacles in their way.

Young Inventor Spotlight — Kenneth Shinozuka

About 48 million people worldwide live with **Alzheimer's disease**. The disease usually affects people 65 years and older. It can cause memory loss and confusion, which means people with the disease cannot remember their surroundings and can easily get lost. Fifteen-year-old Kenneth Shinozuka wanted to help his grandfather and other people living with the disease. Shinozuka designed a special device that attaches to a patient's foot or socks when they are sleeping. If the patient gets out of bed, the device alerts a caregiver by setting off an alarm on their cell phone.

Kenneth designed his innovation to help his grandfather. Do you know someone who needs your help? Even a small innovation can make a huge difference!

Eco Safety

Climate change is causing Earth to get warmer, which is harmful to the environment. Some human activities, such as burning gas and oil, produce air **pollution**, which is a cause of climate change. Trees help to clean the air, but many trees are being cut down or burned in forest fires. Some inventors have thought of ways to help fix the effects of climate change. Moshe Alamaro invented a way to plant trees from the air. He designed pointy containers to carry saplings, or young trees. A plane could carry 100,000 containers at once and drop them to the ground. The containers then rot away and the saplings take root. Using Alamaro's system, as many as one million trees can be planted in one day!

Planting trees is a great way to fight climate change, and it is something anyone can do.

Young Inventor Spotlight   Ari Jónsson

Plastic pollutes the environment because it can take hundreds of years to break down, so it stays in the oceans and soil for a very long time. This pile-up of plastic can be harmful to plants and animals. Ari Jónsson, a student in Iceland, was worried about the plastic problem. To reduce the amount of plastic waste from water bottles, Jónsson designed a water bottle made from plant material. This material dissolves naturally into the soil, and leaves no harmful pollution behind.

Five out of every six water bottles used in the U.S. end up in **landfills** or in our oceans, lakes, and rivers.

Now it's Your Turn!

Inventors, innovators, and engineers follow a set of steps to solve problems and meet needs. These steps are called the Engineering Design Process. The steps in the process can be repeated as many times as needed.

Ask
What is a problem I want to solve or a need I want to meet?

Brainstorm
Write down all possible solutions.

Improve and Communicate
Review your results. Keep improving and testing your solution. Share your results with others.

Plan
Choose the best solution. Write a list of the steps you will follow and materials you will need. Sketch your design.

Create
Build a solution using your plan. Test to see how well it works.

Think Big!

Invention is a process and you can be part of it! The first step is identifying the problem you want to solve or a need you want to meet. Do you see any safety hazards around you? Maybe there is a problem at your home or your school? If you play sports, there may be dangers on the field, on the court, or on the ice. Maybe there is a safety device that you could improve on. When you get involved, you make the world a better place.

Think about a problem you would like to solve. Or choose one of these safety problems:

- Fire hazards at home or school
- Tripping hazards at home or school
- A dangerous area, tool, or object that could harm a child
- Getting lost

Follow the steps in the Engineering Design Process to think big and solve your problem!

Learning More

Books:

Casey, Susan. *Kids Inventing! A Handbook for Young Inventors*. Wiley, 2005

Kenney, Karen. *What Makes Vehicles Safer?* Lerner Publishing Group, 2015

Websites:

This site has biographies of award-winning young inventors. It includes games, resources, and information to encourage new young inventors:
www.lemelson.mit.edu

This site will help you explore how to harness your own creativity:
http://inventivekids.com/

Visit this site for video clips and descriptions of new safety inventions and the inventors who made them:
http://www.abc.net.au/tv/newinventors/inc/categories/ InventionsByCat_SAFETY.htm

Glossary

Alzheimer's disease A disease that causes memory loss, confusion, and changes to personality and mood

black light A special light that makes fluorescent colors glow in the dark

climate change A change in the usual weather of a place

disability A condition that limits a person's movements or activities

engineer A person with scientific training who designs and builds complicated products, machines, systems, or structures

fluorescent Extremely bright or glowing

hearing-impaired Not able to hear well

innovation An improvement of an existing invention

intersection The place where two or more streets meet or cross each other

invention A brand new idea, product, process, or device

landfill An area where waste is buried underground

pollution Substances in the environment that are harmful or toxic

portable Something that is easily carried or moved around

shipwreck A ruined or destroyed ship

solar power Creating power by converting the Sun's rays into electricity

streetcar A vehicle that runs on rails on city streets to carry passengers, similar to a city bus

toxic A material that is poisonous

traits Qualities or characteristics that belong to a person

INDEX

About the Author

Cynthia O'Brien writes non-fiction for children and adults. After working in children's publishing in London, England, for several years, she decided to return to Canada and turn her attention to writing. Cynthia lives in Guelph.